P9-CFF-347

INSIDE THE LUNGS

KARIN HALVORSON, M.D.

Consulting Editor, Diane Craig, M.A./Reading Specialist

A Division of ABDO

ABDO
Publishing Company

VISIT US AT WWW.ABDOPUBLISHING.COM

Published by ABDO Publishing Company, a division of
ABDO, P.O. Box 398166, Minneapolis, Minnesota 55439.
Copyright © 2013 by Abdo Consulting Group, Inc.
International copyrights reserved in all countries. No
part of this book may be reproduced in any form without
written permission from the publisher. Super SandCastle™
is a trademark and logo of ABDO Publishing Company.

Printed in the United States of America,
North Mankato, Minnesota
102012
012013

 PRINTED ON RECYCLED PAPER

Editor: Liz Salzmann
Content Developer: Nancy Tuminelly
Cover and Interior Design: Anders Hanson, Mighty Media
Photo Credits: Shutterstock, Dorling Kindersley RF/Thinkstock,
Colleen Dolphin

Library of Congress Cataloging-in-Publication Data
Halvorson, Karin, 1979-
 Inside the lungs / Karin Halvorson ; consulting editor, Diane Craig,
reading specialist.
    p. cm. -- (Super simple body)
 Audience: 4-10.
 ISBN 978-1-61783-613-8
1. Lungs--Juvenile literature. 2. Respiration--Juvenile literature. I.
Title.
 QP121.H294 2013
 612.2'4--dc23
                        2012030857

Super SandCastle™ books are created by a team of professional
educators, reading specialists, and content developers around five
essential components—phonemic awareness, phonics, vocabulary,
text comprehension, and fluency—to assist young readers as they
develop reading skills and strategies and increase their general
knowledge. All books are written, reviewed, and leveled for guided
reading, early reading intervention, and Accelerated Reader®
programs for use in shared, guided, and independent reading
and writing activities to support a balanced approach to literacy
instruction.

NOTE TO ADULTS

THIS BOOK is all about encouraging
children to learn the science of how
their bodies work! Be there to help
make science fun and interesting for
young readers. Many activities are
included in this book to help children
further explore what they've learned.
Some require adult assistance and/
or permission. Make sure children have
appropriate places where they can do
the activities safely.

Children may also have questions about
what they've learned. Offer help and
guidance when they have questions.
Most of all encourage them to keep
exploring and learning new things!

CONTENTS

YOUR BODY

YOUR LUNGS

You're amazing! So is your body!
Your body has a lot of different parts. Your eyes, ears, brain, stomach, lungs, and heart all work together every day. They keep you moving. Even when you don't realize it.

I t's fun to learn how your body works. From head to toe, your body has some very cool parts. Two of the most exciting are your lungs!

The lungs are special organs. They use air for energy. Lungs help you breathe, laugh, cry, run, and jump!

You have two lungs inside your chest. They are always working to keep you going!

 CAN YOU THINK OF OTHER WAYS THAT YOU USE YOUR LUNGS?

ALL ABOUT THE
LUNGS

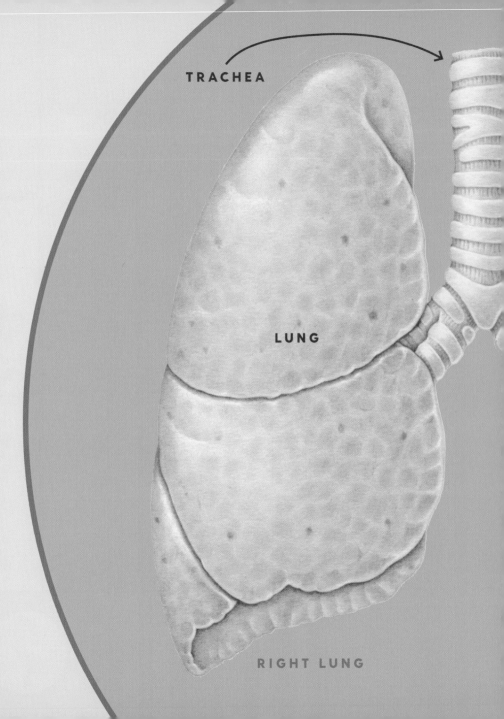

TRACHEA

LUNG

RIGHT LUNG

Your lungs let you breathe. When you breathe in, your lungs fill with air. Your lungs take oxygen from the air and send it into your blood. When you breathe out, your lungs send waste gases from your blood out of your body.

FAST FACT

YOU TAKE ABOUT
22,000 BREATHS
EVERY DAY!

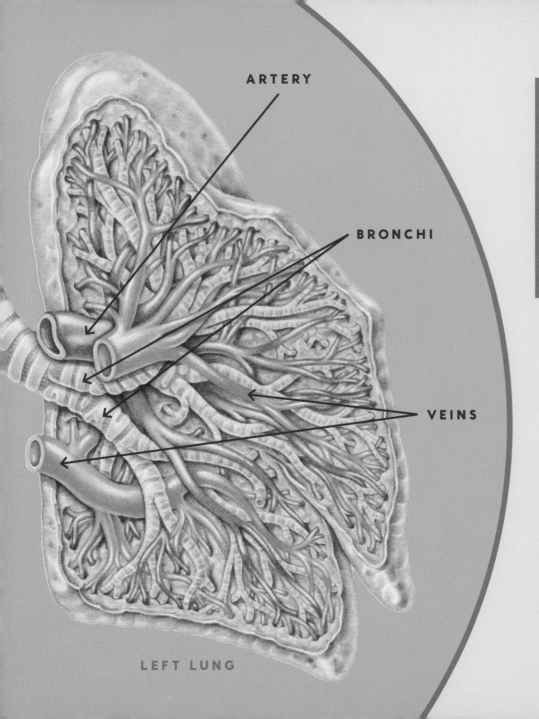

ARTERY

BRONCHI

VEINS

LEFT LUNG

{ FAST FACT }

YOUR LUNGS ARE DIFFERENT SIZES. YOUR LEFT LUNG IS A BIT SMALLER. IT HAS TO MAKE ROOM FOR YOUR HEART!

Your lungs have many arteries and veins. They're tubes that carry blood.

Arteries bring blood into your lungs. Your lungs add oxygen to the blood.

Veins carry the oxygen-rich blood away from your lungs. It goes to your heart. Then your heart pumps it out to the rest of your body!

BREATHE IN

When you breathe in, you push air into your body.

First, the air travels through your nose and mouth to your pharynx (FAR-INGKS). Your pharynx is the back of your throat.

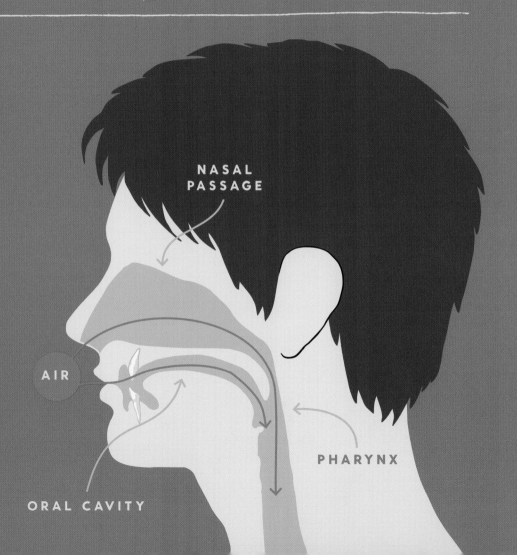

NASAL PASSAGE

AIR

ORAL CAVITY

PHARYNX

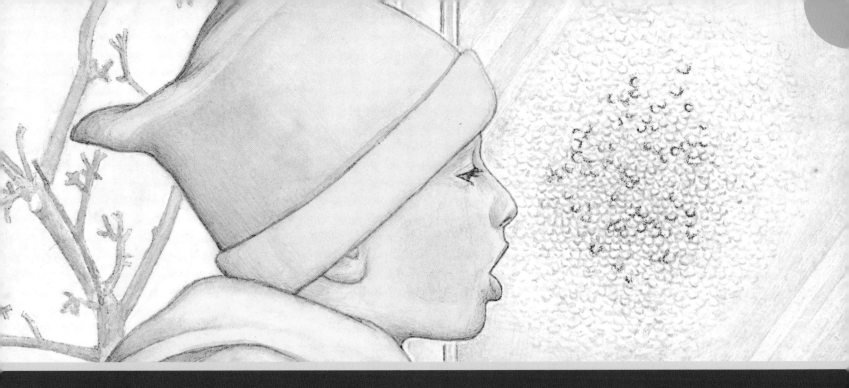

THE AIR APPARENT

Normally you can't see the air you breathe out. But on cold days you can! Do you know why?

The air you breathe out is warm. It also has tiny drops of water in it. The water comes from the moisture in your lungs. The warm, moist air meets the colder air outside your mouth. This turns the water drops into a mist that you can see!

HOT AND HUMID

MAKING AIR WARM AND WET

WHAT YOU NEED: 3 CUPS HOT WATER, 3 TABLESPOONS SALT, LARGE BOWL, GREEN FOOD COLORING, PLASTIC WRAP, LARGE RUBBER BAND, SPOON

HOW TO DO IT

1. Put the salt and warm water in the large bowl. **Squeeze** in six drops of green food coloring.

2. Stir with a spoon.

3. Stretch a large piece of plastic wrap over the bowl. Put a rubber band around the edge to hold it tight.

4. Put the bowl in the refrigerator or another cool, dark place. Check on it after an hour. What changed?

WHAT'S HAPPENING?

Green water droplets collect on the plastic wrap. This is what happens inside your lungs. Your lungs collect the water in the air, just like the plastic wrap.

THE WINDPIPE

Your breath flows through your pharynx into your larynx (LAR-INGKS). Your larynx is also called your voice box.

Then the air goes from your larynx into your trachea (TRAY-KEE-UH). Your trachea is a tube that goes to and from your lungs. It's often called your windpipe.

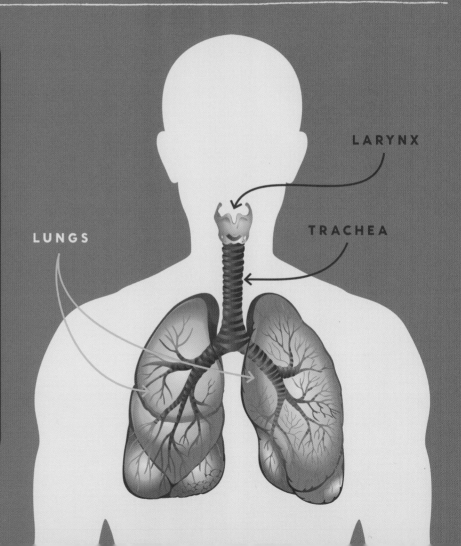

LARYNX

TRACHEA

LUNGS

INSIDE THE TRACHEA

Your trachea is lined with cells that make **mucus**. Dust sticks to the mucus. That way it doesn't get into your lungs.

The cells have hair-like parts, called cilia (SIL-EE-UH). The cilia push the mucus and dust upward. The mucus comes out of your nose or mouth when you **sneeze** or **cough**.

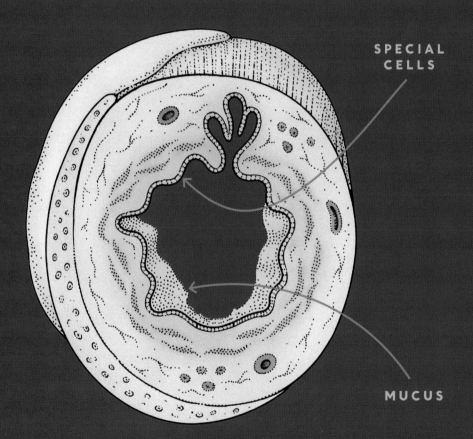

SPECIAL CELLS

MUCUS

TOTALLY
TUBULAR

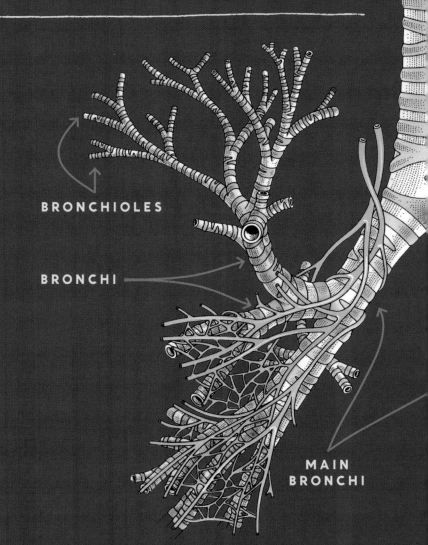

Near the lungs, the trachea splits into two tubes. These tubes are called the main bronchi (BRAHNG-KYE).

The main bronchi split into smaller and smaller bronchi. They look like branches on a tree. The small tubes reach every part of your lungs. When the branches get really small they have a different name. They are called bronchioles (BRAHNG-KEE-OHLZ).

BRONCHIOLES

BRONCHI

MAIN BRONCHI

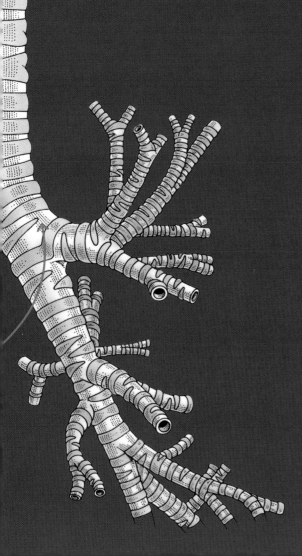

 TRACHEA

THE AIR OUT THERE

The bronchi bring air deep into your lungs. Why do you need air? Because it has a gas called oxygen.

Oxygen is a source of energy. Every action you take requires oxygen. That means you need a lot of air!

Did you know air is more than just oxygen? It's made up of many gases.

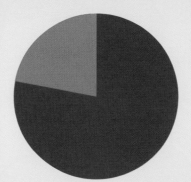

GASES IN THE AIR

78% NITROGEN

21% OXYGEN

1% ARGON AND OTHER GASES

PASSING GASES

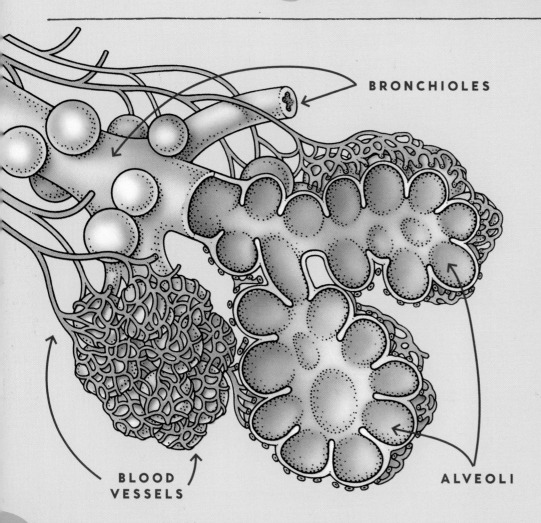

BRONCHIOLES

BLOOD VESSELS

ALVEOLI

There are tiny hollow balls at the ends of the bronchioles. They're called alveoli (AL-VEE-UH-LYE). They let gases pass between your lungs and your blood.

Tiny **blood vessels** surround the alveoli. Oxygen moves through the walls of alveoli into the blood vessels. Your blood brings the oxygen to cells all over your body.

The picture below shows bronchi, bronchioles, and alveoli. The alveoli are like buds at the ends of tree branches.

ALVEOLI ATTACK!

Alveoli are tiny. Each one is the size of a grain of salt!

You have a lot of alveoli. There are more than 300 million in each lung.

If you spread out all your alveoli, they would probably cover the floor of your classroom!

MAKING
ENERGY

Your cells use oxygen to make energy. Have you noticed that you breathe harder after you've been active? Being active takes more energy than resting. To make the extra energy, your cells need more oxygen than usual. That's why you breathe harder and faster.

WHAT KINDS OF ACTIVITIES DO YOU DO?

WASTE

When your cells use oxygen, they create another gas. It's called carbon dioxide (**KAHR-BUHN DYE-AHK-SIDE**).

Carbon dioxide is a waste gas. It stays in your blood until it reaches the **blood vessels** around the alveoli. It passes into the alveoli. Then you can breathe it out!

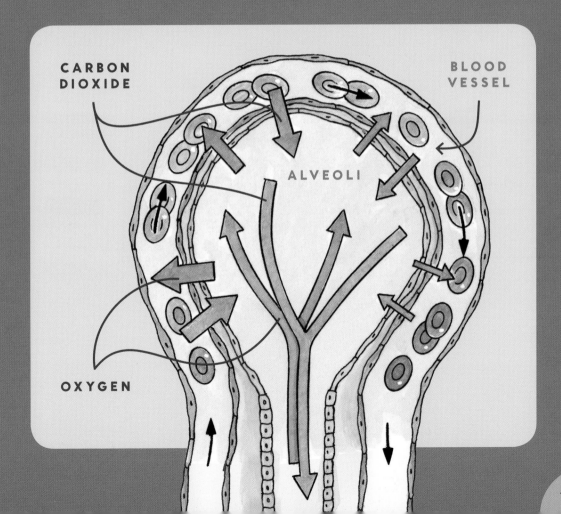

CARBON DIOXIDE

BLOOD VESSEL

ALVEOLI

OXYGEN

BREATH RATE

HOW MUCH AIR DO YOU NEED?

WHAT YOU NEED: **CHAIR, PENCIL, PAPER, STOPWATCH**

HOW TO DO IT

1 Sit or lie still. Count how many breaths you take in 30 seconds. A breath is breathing in and out one time. Write the number down. How do you feel? Do you have a lot of energy?

2 Walk for five minutes. Then count your breaths for 30 seconds again. Write the number down. Was it higher this time?

3 Run as fast as you can for five minutes. Then count your breaths for 30 seconds. What number did you get this time? Are you tired now?

4 Keep going with other activities you like. Count your breaths after doing jumping jacks, dancing, or playing basketball. When do you take the most breaths?

WHAT'S HAPPENING?

The more active you are, the more energy you use. So your body needs more oxygen to make more energy. You breathe faster to bring more oxygen into your body.

BREATHE OUT

There is a large muscle right below your lungs. It's called your diaphragm (**DYE-UH-FRAM**). Your diaphragm moves up and down.

When you breathe in, it moves down. This sucks air into your lungs.

When you breathe out, it moves up. This **squeezes** air out of your lungs.

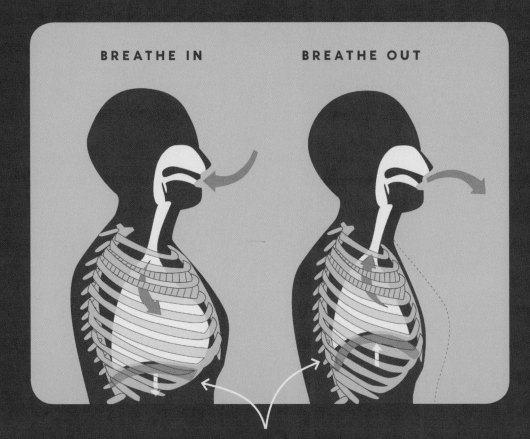

BREATHE IN   BREATHE OUT

DIAPHRAGM

Breathing out removes carbon dioxide from your body.

It goes up through your bronchioles and bronchi. Then it flows through your trachea and larynx. Finally, it exits through your nose or mouth!

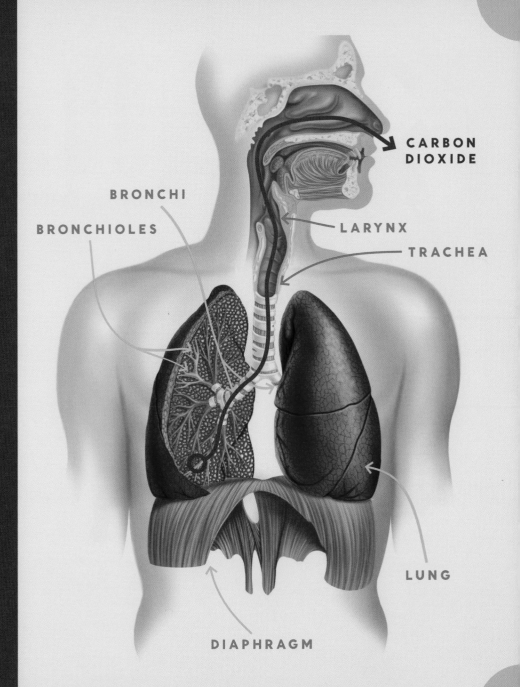

CARBON DIOXIDE

BRONCHI

BRONCHIOLES

LARYNX

TRACHEA

LUNG

DIAPHRAGM

FULL OF HOT AIR

HOW MUCH AIR CAN YOU HOLD?

WHAT YOU NEED: 8 × 8-INCH BAKING PAN, 1-GALLON PLASTIC JUG, WATER, 6-INCH (16 CM) RUBBER TUBE

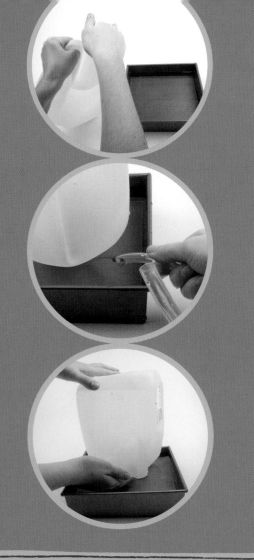

HOW TO DO IT

1. Fill the jug with water. Fill the baking pan half way with water. Cover the top of the jug with your hand. Turn the jug upside down into the pan. Take your hand away when the top of the jug is underwater. The water won't come out!

2. Put one end of the tube in the jug. Make sure the jug's opening stays underwater. Take a deep breath and blow into the other end of the tube. Blow as long as you can without breathing in again.

3. Put your hand under the opening of the jug. Turn the jug right side up.

4. The jug isn't full anymore, right? The space in the jug above the water is how much air you had in your lungs!

WHAT'S HAPPENING?

When you breathed into the jug, the air needed somewhere to go. So it forced water out to make room. It made a space big enough for one breath.

VOCAL MOTION

When you breathe, air flows through your **vocal** folds. They're also called vocal cords.

Your vocal folds open to let the air through. When you speak or sing, your vocal folds **vibrate**. They open and close quickly. That creates vibrations in the air flowing through them. Those vibrations are your voice!

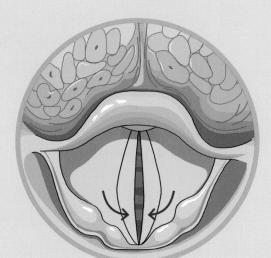

CLOSED VOCAL FOLDS

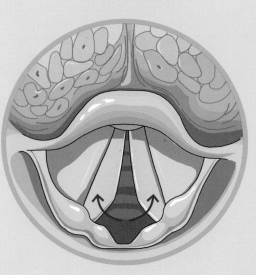

OPEN VOCAL FOLDS

VIBRATIONS IN AIR

SORE THROAT?

Have you ever had a sore throat? It hurts when you swallow. Sometimes you lose your voice!

Sore throats can happen for a lot of reasons. You may have a cold. Or it may be from shouting loudly for a long time.

If you have a sore throat, it means your throat is **swollen.** When your larynx swells, it is hard to speak or sing!

SING IT LOUD

HOW DOES YOUR VOICE WORK?

WHAT YOU NEED: **BALLOON**

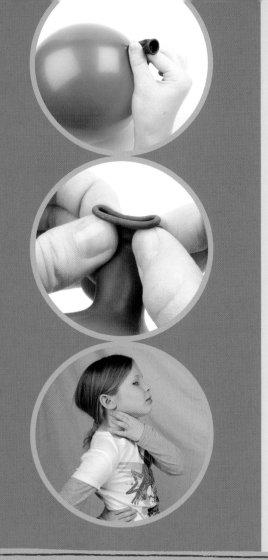

HOW TO DO IT

1. Blow up a balloon.

2. Pinch the opening to keep the air in the balloon.

3. Use your fingers to stretch the opening. Just a little bit of air comes out. The edges of the opening **vibrate**. You hear a high-pitched squeaking noise.

4. Put one hand on your neck under your jaw. Hum as low as you can. Then hum as high as you can. Can you feel the vibration?

WHAT'S HAPPENING?

When you let air out of the balloon, the edges of the opening vibrate. The vibration makes a sound. Your lungs are like the balloon. Your **vocal** folds are like the balloon's opening.

MAKE A LUNG

SEE HOW BREATHING WORKS!

WHAT YOU NEED: 2-LITER PLASTIC BOTTLE, RULER, MARKER, SCISSORS, REGULAR BALLOON, SMALL BALLOON, STRAW, 2 RUBBER BANDS, CLAY

HOW TO DO IT

1. Measure 5 inches (13 cm) from the bottom of the bottle. Draw a line. Cut off the bottom of the plastic bottle under the line. **Discard** the bottom. Keep the top part.

2. Tie a knot in the stem of the regular-sized balloon. Cut off the end of the balloon opposite from the stem. Stretch the balloon over the end of the bottle. Make sure the knot is on the outside. Put a rubber band around the edge to hold it tight.

3. Put one end of the straw in the small balloon. Use a rubber band to hold the balloon in place. Put the small balloon in the bottle with the straw sticking out. Use clay to seal the top of the bottle around the straw.

WHAT'S HAPPENING?

You made a model of breathing! The small balloon is the lung. The balloon across the bottom of the bottle is the diaphragm. Pull the knot to make it move up and down. Watch the small balloon inflate.

BLOOD VESSEL – one of the tubes that carry blood throughout the body.

COUGH – the act or sound of suddenly forcing air out of your lungs.

DISCARD – to throw away.

MUCUS – a slippery sticky substance produced by the body.

SNEEZE – the act or sound of suddenly forcing air out through your nose or mouth.

SQUEEZE – to press or grip something tightly.

SWOLLEN – larger than normal.

VIBRATE – to make very small, quick movements back and forth.

VOCAL – having to do with the voice.

GLOSSARY